Rena Te Sueltz

MY WAY
findings & wisdom

BoD - Books on Demand
Norderstedt 2020

Renate & Uwe H. Sültz
Bücher von A bis Z

Bibliografische Information durch die Deutsche Nationalbibliothek
Die Deutsche Nationalbibliothek verzeichnet diese Publikation in der
Deutschen Nationalbibliografie; detaillierte bibliografische Daten
sind im Internet über http://dnb.dnb.de abrufbar.

© RENATE SUELTZ

Herstellung und Verlag:
BoD – Books on Demand, Norderstedt
ISBN 9-78375-2-60518-1

<u>MY WAY</u> - There is a lot of literature on Lao-Tse. But basically we know very little about his life.

What we can tell about him comes from legendary tales. Lao-Tse was the Imperial archivist of the Chou (dynasty). He strove to be only in secret. In Tibet I learned a lot from the monks. Among other things, that this wise man did not want to make a name for himself. He lived in Tschou for a long time.

Foreseeing that Chou was about to decay, Lao-Tze went into the distance. Finally he reached the border pass. The border commander, the

monks told me, was called Yin Hi. He asked Lao-Tse to pass on his knowledge in the form of a book.

The book that followed was written in two parts. He wrote down his thoughts in 5000 or more words. Then he disappeared and no one has ever known where he is. Many suspect that he lived to be 160-200 years old. According to tradition, he died around 350 BC. The teaching of Lao-Tse refers to the Tao and Te it means purity and calm. Originally Tao (the way) meant: principle, speaking the word, meaning, world law, reason. Furthermore, philosophers think to interpret the Tao as follows: way and cycle of the universe. I've been advocating this theory for a long time. It could also mean "harmonious change" in nature. Bloom and bloom. Eternally creative path. Beginning and end of all being. Everything that exists comes from the Tao and ultimately returns to it.

The Tao includes and generates Yin and Yang. They are the two primal forces. The dark, resting, signing, feminine yin and the light, generating, masculine yang. The creative, alternating forces of yin and yang should shape the recurring, annual cycle of nature in constant change.

Lao-Tse described a transcendent Tao that cannot be explored and a phenomenal Tao that is recognizable and nameable. The Tao unites pure and practical reason at the same time.

It is said that whoever attains the Tao is a saint.

Something about immortality

I learned something about the subject of immortality in Tibet. My study trip took me there, although this topic shouldn't be relevant to me as a budding journalist. Still, I felt it was important for me to find out about it.

Immortality is firmly anchored in Taoism. I kept thinking about how a human being could become immortal. I was fascinated by observing the monks in Tibet. With what humility and superiority they shaped the hours of the day. Prayer and meditation come first. There are numerous books about Taoism that I really devoured. As I read I was constantly overcome by a feeling of confusion and frustration, but mostly fascination. I believe that a great many people have difficulty really understanding the Tao. Back then in Tibet I was repeatedly told that there was a secret that would not be revealed to everyone. For a long time I could not tell which books on the Tao were not so good or really good.

I kept searching, according to Taoist tradition, and now I knew that Lao-Tse was the true, great thinker. Well, I spoke of meditation and I can say that the Chinese do that most of the time. Mainly, they promote their health, expand awareness and promote the development of PSI strength.

Meditation in silence and the healing arts of the Chinese

In meditation, Taoists prefer certain techniques that affect each other's mind and body. Each of us would benefit greatly from meditating regularly. Now again to immortality. Don't we all want to be ageless and immortal? Yes, I think so, because people are very interested in the universe and the origin of life. In Buddhism, heaven represents the pure land of Buddha.

The Chinese have different spiritual points of view, but basically there is a common foundation.

There are, for example, the same techniques that enable us to cultivate body and mind and to overcome the barriers of the material world. Also, to attain eternal life and unlock its secrets.

In China, a long time ago, there was a sage who was desperate to prove that man can really achieve immortality. He thought a regular way of life was essential. Only this claim can neither be confirmed nor refuted. I would also like to rediscover the Chinese healing arts, for myself and for my husband. The given way of life would then have to be practiced. But we've been practicing this for a few years now. In the field of psychotherapy, the holistic health teachings of the Chinese and their healing arts are particularly important. The theories of immortality have been handed down from generation to generation for thousands of years.

If one wants to represent the view of the Chinese, one can only meditate in a quiet place and while sitting. There are supposed to be 30 different positions that guarantee a promising meditation. The so-called "stillness" can equally include rest and movement. The aim is to achieve absolute silence, outside as well as inside. In this state, as far as I know, longevity and health should be cultivated.

Since we as authors and journalists often work late into the night, we need a lot of rest and sleep afterwards. In this way, our vital forces are renewed during sleep. Lao-Tzu once said: "All things return to their own roots."

Principles of Taoism are described in "the clear silent sutra". These are derived from observations and imitations of nature. Spiritual development and maturity are only cultivated in absolute silence. This development should be the way to pre-heavenly maturity. I firmly believe that it is. In absolute silence it is possible to see many things in a different light. I also think that wisdom can only be obtained in absolute silence.

Findings and principles

Life is very precious. For many of us, the day is one rush hour. Everything just has to go very quickly. But I couldn't find my way anymore under constant time pressure. Life is never given to us a second time. I wanted to protect this precious life from now on. Today I managed to get out of the treadmill of everyday life. I thank God again and again for giving us paradise on earth. He only wanted the best for us. Outside, in the silence of the wonderful nature, I am always freed from all negative thoughts. Today I realize what it means to be in paradise.

Nevertheless, I always feel at the mercy of the hectic pace of this time. It often takes a while to get on the right path. All my life so far, I pulled myself together again and again when the work and the stress wanted to drag me into the abyss. I raised three children alone, still went to work and made sure that the children had a good lunch on the table every day. I loved the three and also life. I often said to myself: "Hold on, the children are happy, that's something wonderful and the most important thing. I persevered and enjoyed seeing my sons develop and become logical, healthy and lovable people. "

Even if I often don't find a place to dawdle
and do nothing in this day and age, I force
myself to meditate in a quiet place.

A hectic pace is not good for us.

We just work and rush.

Let's take courage

and go out into nature.

From now on I got out of the everyday process regularly.
As we work as freelance authors in our own four walls or
in the various offices we have set up, it was easy
for me to find a place to retreat.

"Why now?" I thought. I set up a small, separate reading
corner. When I hit rock bottom again, I retreated there.
I read my favorite books until I had enough energy again.

It was entirely up to me how I planned my daily routine.
I never wanted to get addicted to stress again.

Now I made sure that I had enough leeway for various tasks that I had to do during the day.

I had to reserve larger time packages for this. I filled the rest of the free time with creative things. Now I never felt like I missed anything again.

Take some rest

We all have enough time to organize our daily lives. If someone says to me that they don't have time, I don't believe them. There is a sunset and a sunrise.

In between there is enough leeway that can be sensibly divided and designed. But in such a way that there is time for the most important things. It is the phases of rest that we need in order to maintain our emotional balance, to find inner peace and to organize our thoughts. This time should be included in our daily routine.

Can live, let live.

Want to live, be happy.

Accept, no longer hate.

Pure in heart and mind.

Regardless of whether at work or at home, I don't want to and can't expect much anymore. Among other things, health problems also play a role. But the main thing I had to do was create an island of calm. The inner peace and serenity that

I feel every time is very important for my soul life and gives me strength to cope with everyday life. At these moments, I turn off my PC and my cell phone. I stand by the window and look out. I can switch off my thoughts completely. Or I sit down in my comfortable wing chair and read for half an hour. Everyone can choose how they plan their rest periods. A quiet place is important.

There must be absolute calm. What each individual does then is up to them. I don't know what others are feeling, but always after this period of rest I have a wonderful feeling of balance that I had never known before. I stay calm even when others are hectic around me.

Take your time, just let go.

Forget the crushing monotony.

Your longing for peace is great.

The hustle and bustle will pass.

Find the silence and free yourself.

Take your leisure time.

Problems are now the same.

You have found inner peace.

Be happy

I never want to be unhappy. To do this, I had to learn to find inner peace. Only now in my old age do I realize that life is true reality. When you are young you don't know anything about the world, you hardly think about life and everything that goes with it.

I often ask myself why there are problems. Almost all of us have a habit of viewing the smallest discrepancy as a problem. In my opinion there are no problems. Why don't we try to reshape the world with just positive thoughts? I think it would work. All negative thoughts would then be smoke and mirrors, and there would be no problems at all. Happy people usually have good characters and a positive outlook on life. Everything I do, I do with all my heart and with joy. My husband and I respect each other for who we are. We're different, but that's also important. Through this partnership behavior in our marriage, we feel happiness anew every day.

The happiness that I found

you are my dear man

I only knew fear.

Nothing nicer I can feel.

Just a simple smile, when we offer it to other people, can make the person who has that smile happy. I practice it every day and it makes not only others happy but also me.

I keep myself far away from people who give me bad vibrations. I can feel immediately whether it is a good or a bad person. It may sound arrogant, but it's not good for my soul. I no longer accept anything in the world blindly, but neither do I categorically reject anything. In everything I do or think, I take small steps towards the truth. The truth about life.

Live your life, get wise.

Always stay with you.

Send good thoughts on the journey

leave the negative here.

Learn to be free to think.

Find peace, quiet, and quiet.

Try not to direct others

all that matters is your will.

When I see everything that is in the world and what happens as a gift, I have understood what life is. There are many things that I have lived through in my life and which I have thought about. They still have their place, but they are definitely no longer consistent. I've changed, and so have circumstances. I let go of what no longer belongs to me and held onto what I really love. I've always looked for happiness in big, spectacular things. Now I see it in the simplest of things.

It has to go on and on. We cannot know in advance whether the paths we are treading are always the right ones or the wrong ones.

I went into my rose garden and took a deep breath of the scent of this divine plant …

The rose is a symbol of love.

Its smell is beguiling.

I feel good around her.

Can never have enough of her.

It grows proudly in my garden

the most beautiful flower far and wide.

Dearest i will wait for you

because our time will come.

<u>And slowly my thoughts became clearer and I opened the door in my heart …</u>

Finally let happiness in your house,

then grief and pain pass.

The negative flies out

Love comes into your heart.

It doesn't take much to be happy

just try to understand

The positive is your goal.

Happiness is so close, you will see it.

I will enjoy every moment in life, because the beautiful moments just fly by. Small messages that I received in life were and are always a sign of fate. I've learned to recognize them. Money alone doesn't make me happy either. On the contrary, it can be very lonely.

Until my death I will remain positive and even in old age, if I can achieve this, I will enjoy the moment. With full awareness I have turned my attention away from the things that should not be. Instead, I focused intensely on what should be.

Enjoy the moment in life.

Do your soul good.

Not what you do is in vain.

Go through life in good spirits.

Look only on the essentials, enjoy life.

Cherish the moment and live today.

Stay positive, try to give it your all.

Feel happiness ... without being gripped by constraints

To be free also means to be happy. Be free from all constraints and do what I want. I have a safe home and feel particularly lucky; And I know where I belong When I was just in love, I had butterflies in my stomach. Everyone has probably felt that feeling before. I also have butterflies in my stomach when I wake up in the morning and there is someone next to me who belongs to me.

Each of us is happy to be caught, no matter what. Turn your back on unpleasant things. It is a good feeling and creates a certain feeling of happiness. I've learned and just let myself go. I just put all worries aside. But that doesn't mean that I don't do important things. It has nothing to do with it. I just enjoy the happiness that I am currently experiencing.

Enjoy everything beautiful in this world.

Spend your time wisely.

Go through the world positively.

Your goal is not far anymore.

<u>Treat all things with respect, just as you want to be respected</u>

I approach all things in life with respect. I have found that everything is precious. Every single part that exists in my life is a link in a long chain. I've learned to look at everything carefully. Eventually it became the beginning of a conscious life. My life partner is my second me and our minds are so interconnected that everything else is like a speck of dust.

In the end I decided on the "WAY OF JOY". With friends and those who want no harm and will do no harm to me. With them I will go to the end of being.

Don't forget to live in peace.

Please only do what you like.

You should give zest for life and joy.

Learn what lights up your mind.

Enjoy your existence with all your might.

Look how the leaves blow in the wind.

You made a big part of the way.

Soon you will be ready and able to understand.

Wisdom doesn't just fly to you.

You have to study and see things.

Acquire peace and tranquility.

With an enlightened heart you will go.

<u>What I broadcast, I got back. The love I gave in this life is given to me too …</u>

I gave you a lot of love.

We cried and laughed.

I wanted to experience happiness with you.

Caressed your body gently.

It's still beautiful to this day.

It should always be like that.

We will never part.

Our thoughts are wise and pure.

I like to remember what it was like

it is always in my mind.

I was happy when I saw you

Now know what true love means.

Enjoy the silence, seek the peace and you will feel great happiness

A while ago I was afraid to be alone. But I found out that there is a solution to this. At least once I told myself not to think about anything, not to speak. The silence around me became the only agony. I told myself to be quiet, and then something unusual happened. Old habits and bad feelings arose that made the silence restless. I took refuge in activities because I was not used to this silence. I found it bad and depressing.

I thought about it and realized that I suddenly found this silence to be unique. I came to life and found this a wonderful challenge. In fact, it should become the focus of everything I did. But again I wondered why people are unhappy and why the world is so chaotic.

Don't worry too much.

Dream your dream.

Otherwise you will quickly falter

And you will hardly be happy.

Don't listen to what others are saying.

Think 'well and be silent'.

You have to dare something new

Show them the cold shoulder '.

In the HERE and NOW, you should live there,

and go through life positively.

You shouldn't take but give

and always see only the GOOD.

Life is not child's play.

Often times it is difficult to take.

We take it courageously and quietly.

We also have to dare to take difficult steps.

The theater, which is called "Life",

demands all strength from us.

But we fight and mostly notice

that we somehow made it.

So say yes to life

then you will be happy.

You have to give everything again

remember you are not alone

Be satisfied with what has been given to you.

Gain wisdom and sharpen your thinking.

Say yes to this beautiful life

Eternal life will be given to you by God.

Life is a gift, we should respect it

I consider myself a gift of life. But also without being arrogant towards others. As we know, matter is transitory. Actually nothing belongs to me because everything is just borrowed. There is absolutely nothing I can consider my own. I've always been aware of it. It helped me see life from a completely different perspective. When I understood all of this, I could finally say yes to life. I also realized that all people are absolutely the same. Skin color and status are irrelevant. Everything is unimportant. I now know what is really important. I have internalized who I really am. I have discovered what a wonderful gift it is to be here as a person. Yes, the daily awakening and participating in life is more than a gift for which I am infinitely grateful.

Life is not eternal.

Time passes calmly.

To heaven we will float

The goal is not far.

So live now, it's so important.

Do what you have to do

Take yourself seriously

And feel happiness and lust.

Belief is part of life.

Belief in yourself.

Never let yourself be deprived of happiness.

You hold it tight in your hands.

Make up your own mind, because you will do the right thing

I make very few decisions with my mind, but with my heart. Most of the time, the decision is made before I even think about it or say it. If I act spontaneously and intuitively, this happens automatically and mostly by itself. If my decisions are correct, the causes that set them are always correct.

What is a task for? To get done, of course. However, I can only consider a task completed when I have finished it. I follow this rule and every single project will be a success. It may sound arrogant again, but I want to be successful. Not just once, but forever. It was worth it for me. It will also be worthwhile for anyone else who knows the rules and obeys them.

After all, who doesn't want to leave the field as a winner? To do this, you have to remember a principle that has always brought me success and still does. In any case, it is useful to me in many situations. I see myself as a winner on all levels in spirit. I can feel very clearly that I have reached my goal. Often it is not clear to me, but winners and losers are usually already determined at the start. The way I approach things logically has an impact on the course and outcome of the matter itself. In any case, I've decided to be a winner. I firmly believe it will turn out that way.

It is important to realize

the way you have to go.

It's good not to run away.

No, hold on until the end.

Did you know your soul

then you don't have to say anything more.

Be curious about what's to come.

Dare to dare to do something.

Do you see what is important for you

then you have won a lot.

Fate won't let you down.

Nothing is taken from you.

Optimize your awareness - Invest in revitalizing intuition

We all have this ability within us. I also had to activate it first. Unfortunately, I almost forgot. However, in order to get useful results, I learned to listen to my feelings. From now on I acted intuitively and the results were really impressive. My mind can only store a small part of information. What the mind or the memory can hold on to can be called up again at any time.

In any case, the subconscious can store almost anything. Our mind has no access to the level on which our experiences are stored, but memory does. I know today that my mind is identical to this level. It was right that I made the decisions from the heart. I trusted my feeling when it said "yes". In any case, I tried to optimize the natural ability of my intuition.

Try to let go of what can no longer be held

Although it is actually easy, I found it very difficult to banish from my thinking unpleasant, even cruel experiences, but also things that I could not have changed. I had to let go at all costs. I had to save my family, my life and my soul. I did and this was the right path. It was my path that could only lead me to happiness in my life under this condition. I did it for good. I also decided to go to Tibet to substantiate my findings and to learn even more.

I think it's not just about letting go, it's about why we can't let go. I was scared and longed for something I couldn't get. Today I am a happy person and glad I did that. I am a happy person, only think of beautiful things, am creative and live life. My experiences in Tibet are to be published in a third part.

Go your way, be smart.

Let go of what is destroying your happiness.

A new life is ready for you.

The world is now finally yours.

Get rid of bad things.

They only block your life.

Only in this way can new things begin.

It will give you satisfaction.

Say yes to yourself at last, look inside yourself.

Go the way that life knows you.

Happiness accompanies you, does not leave you alone.

You finally understand what life means.

I have often asked myself when did thinking begin in people? What happened before we could even think. What did I do or where was I before the first thought arose in my brain? Again I realized that I am something extraordinary, or that everyone is extraordinary. This applies to all people on this planet, maybe even in the entire universe.

I and my fellow human beings can call themselves all-minds. This is a great gift and we should be guided by it. I did it after gaining a lot of knowledge.

I am constantly being guided by this force. Much is now possible that I previously felt was impossible. What broke out of me transformed me and carried out an absolute renewal in me.

Take a lot of time for your thoughts.

If they are positive, they purify your mind.

No brooding and no wavering

pointing you the wrong way.

Do what is best for you.

Let go of what torments you.

Not a bit you miss.

The here and now only counts.

I would like to thank my readers

Rena Te Sueltz